W9-DFQ-053

MADAM C.J. WALKER

INVENTOR AND MILLIONAIRE

Famous African Americans

Patricia and Fredrick McKissack

Enslow Elementary
an imprint of
Enslow Publishers, Inc.
40 Industrial Road
Box 398
Berkeley Heights, NJ 07922
USA
http://www.enslow.com

To Alfreda Vance

Enslow Elementary, an imprint of Enslow Publishers, Inc.

Enslow Elementary® is a registered trademark of Enslow Publishers, Inc.

Copyright © 2013 by Enslow Publishers, Inc.

Original edition published as *Madam C. J. Walker: Self-Made Millionaire* in 1992.

Library of Congress Cataloging-in-Publication Data

McKissack, Pat, 1944-
   Madam C.J. Walker : inventor and millionaire / Patricia and Fredrick McKissack.
     p. cm. — (Famous African Americans)
   Includes bibliographical references and index.
   Summary: "A simple biography about Madam CJ Walker for early readers"—Provided by publisher.
   ISBN 978-0-7660-4105-9
   1. Walker, C. J., Madam, 1867-1919. 2. African American women executives—Biography. 3. Cosmetics industry—United States—History. 4. Women millionaires—United States—Biography. 5. African Americans—Biography. I. McKissack, Fredrick. II. Title.
   HD9970.5.C672W3563 2013
   338.7'66855092—dc23
   [B]
                             2012014358

Future editions
Paperback ISBN 978-1-4644-0201-2
ePUB ISBN 978-1-4645-1114-1
PDF ISBN 978-1-4646-1114-8

Printed in the United States of America
082012 Lake Book Manufacturing, Inc., Melrose Park, IL

10 9 8 7 6 5 4 3 2 1

Photo Credits: Library of Congress, pp. 14 (left), 16; Madam C. J. Walker Collection, Indiana Historical Society, pp. 1, 3, 7, 14 (right), 18, 20.

Illustration Credits: Michael Bryant, pp. 4, 8, 10, 13.

Cover Illustration: Madam C. J. Walker Collection, Indiana Historical Society

Series Consultant:
Russell Adams, PhD
Emeritus Professor
Afro-American Studies
Howard University

CONTENTS

Many freed slaves in the South worked in the same fields they had worked in when they were slaves.

CHAPTER 1
CHRISTMAS BABY

Before the **Civil War**, Owen and Minerva Breedlove were **slaves**. They worked in the cotton fields on a large Louisiana **plantation**. When the war ended in 1865, so did slavery. Millions of African Americans were freed, including the Breedloves and their children, Louvenia, Alexander, James, and Owen Jr.

Freedom was just about all the family had. Owen and Minerva did not have money, jobs, or a home. All they knew how to do was farm. But they had no land.

The Breedloves did what many other slaves did. They became sharecroppers. They rented land from their old master and farmed it. Owen and Minerva worked long, hard hours on their rented farm. Still they stayed poor. Most of what they earned went to pay back the landowner for seeds and food. There was no way to get ahead.

Owen and Minerva Breedlove were going to have another child. Christmas was not far away. There was no money for gifts. Two days before Christmas in 1867, Sarah Breedlove was born. The family called her their Christmas baby. They had high hopes for this child. She was born free!

Sarah Breedlove was born in this small cabin in Louisiana. She grew up to be the country's first female self-made millionaire.

Sarah and her sister worked hard. They made money by washing other people's clothes.

CHAPTER 2

MOVING UP THE RIVER

· ·

Life was hard for Sarah and her family. It got even worse. There were many deadly diseases. Her parents got very sick and died. By 1875, Sarah was an **orphan**.

Seven-year-old Sarah went to live with her married sister. Louvenia tried to take care of her as best she could. But the cotton crops failed year after year. They needed money to live.

Sarah's brother Alex decided to move across the river to Vicksburg, Mississippi. After a while, Louvenia and her husband and Sarah moved there, too. The two young women took in laundry to make a living. Soon young Sarah married Moses McWilliams so she could "have a home of her own." On June 6, 1885, Sarah's daughter, Lelia, was born. About three years later, Moses died.

In the 1800s there were many steamboats on the Mississippi River. Sarah enjoyed watching them.

Vicksburg was a river town. Sarah watched riverboats float up and down the river. She decided it was time to move on, too. Sarah moved to St. Louis, Missouri, in 1889.

Soon Sarah had a good laundry business there. But she wondered if life would ever be better for her and Lelia.

Sarah worked hard so Lelia could go to school. Lelia was bright and enjoyed reading. Sarah sent her to Knoxville College in Tennessee. Meanwhile, Sarah wasn't happy doing laundry. She wanted to do more with her life.

In 1904, Sarah went to hear Margaret Murray Washington speak at a meeting of the **National Association of Colored Women** in St. Louis. Margaret Murray Washington was the wife of Booker T. Washington, the most well known black leader of the time. She gave a great speech about the rewards of hard work.

Sarah made up her mind. She was going to improve her life.

CHAPTER 3
THE WALKER PLAN

There were not many products for black women's hair problems. Sarah's hair was thin and dry. Some of it was falling out. Sarah decided to make a **hair grower** to use on her own hair. It worked. Her hair grew longer and thicker.

Lelia was away at college. Sarah had married again, but she divorced her husband. There was nothing keeping Sarah in St. Louis. So she moved to Denver, where her brother Owen's wife and four daughters lived.

Sarah got a job in a drugstore. At night she worked on her hair products. Soon, Sarah began selling her goods from door to door. Black women were happy to have something that made their hair look nice. Sarah's sales were so good, she hired women to help sell door-to-door, too.

Sarah went from house to house telling women about her hair products. Soon her business started to grow.

Sarah's husband C.J. helped with advertising. This is an ad for some of Madam Walker's hair products.

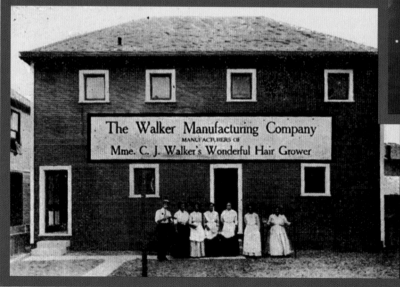

Sarah had known Charles Joseph (C. J.) Walker back in St. Louis. Now he lived in Denver, too. Their friendship soon grew into love. On January 4, 1906, Charles and Sarah were married. From that time on, she called herself Madam C. J. Walker.

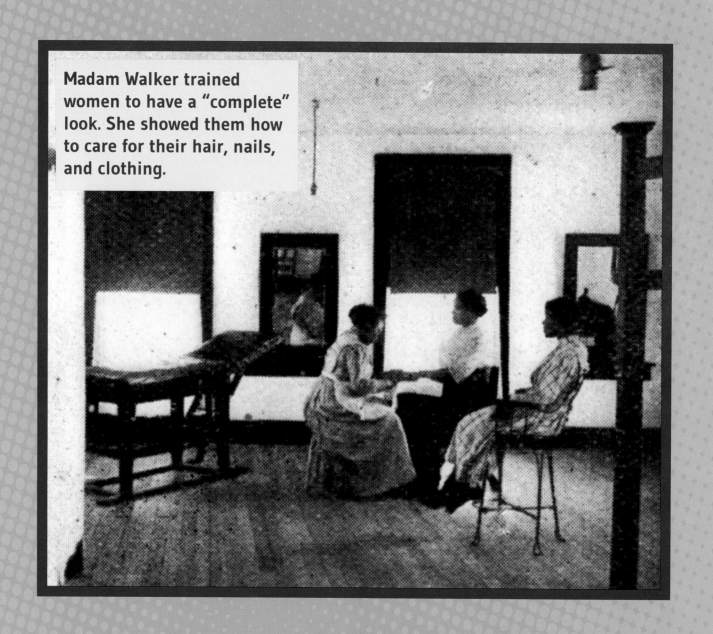

Madam Walker trained women to have a "complete" look. She showed them how to care for their hair, nails, and clothing.

CHAPTER 4
THE WALKER TEAM

When Lelia **graduated** from college, she came to help her mother. In 1908, Madam Walker and her daughter opened Lelia College in Pittsburgh, Pennsylvania. They trained women in the Walker hair care plan. Women who graduated from the school were called hair culturists.

First the culturist washed the woman's hair. Madam Walker's hair grower was added. Then the customer's hair was pressed with a hot comb and curled.

In 1910, Madam Walker built her first **factory** in Indianapolis, Indiana. Right away she hired people to help build a strong business. Lawyers Robert Lee Brokenburr and Freeman Briley Ransom managed the company. Violet Davis Reynolds was Madam Walker's secretary and good friend. They traveled together. They showed other black women that they could start businesses, too.

Black women loved the idea! In 1910, most black women made from $2 to $10 a week. Madam Walker's hair culturists were making $20 a week or more.

A year after moving to Indianapolis, the company had 950 salespeople. The company earned $1,000 a month. Madam Walker put the money back into the business. By 1918, her company was earning about $250,000 a year. Madam Walker made history by becoming America's first female **self-made millionaire**—white or black!

Madam Walker had enough money to buy several cars. Although she had a driver, she sometimes drove herself.

CHAPTER 5
FOR A GOOD CAUSE

Madam Walker used her money to make life better for her family and people who worked for her. She also gave to churches, schools, hospitals, and other good causes.

Madam Walker and her daughter, who had changed her name to A'Lelia, were interested in **civil rights**. At that time the country was **segregated**. The laws kept black people and white people apart. Blacks and whites couldn't ride buses or trains together. They couldn't go to the same schools.

Once Madam Walker went to a white theater. They charged her more money because she was black. First she sued the theater. Then she built the Walker Building, a block-long business center in downtown Indianapolis. Inside, there was a new movie theater where black and white people could sit together.

Madam Walker used her success to help other African Americans. Here she is at the opening of a YMCA for African Americans. Standing next to her is black leader Booker T. Washington.

Most jobs weren't open to blacks. Madam Walker spoke to groups all over the country. She believed black people should start more businesses in their own neighborhoods. Then there would be more jobs for African Americans.

In 1913, A'Lelia moved to Harlem, a mostly black neighborhood in New York City. She wanted her mother to move there. Harlem was becoming the center of black life.

Finally Madam Walker agreed that New York was the place to live. In 1916, she left Indianapolis. But the Walker Factory stayed there. F. B. Ransom and Alice Kelly were left in charge. Alice Kelly knew Madam Walker's secret formula. Madam Walker and A'Lelia were the only other people who knew the formula at that time.

Madam Walker had worked hard all her life. Now her health was poor. Her doctors told her to slow down, but she did not know how to rest. Madam Walker traveled around the country giving speeches and opening new beauty shops.

Sarah Breedlove Walker, known as Madam C. J. Walker, died on May 25, 1919. She was fifty-one years old.

WORDS TO KNOW

civil rights—The rights of a free people, including the right to vote.

civil war—A war fought within one country.

factory—A place where products to be sold are made.

graduate—To finish the required course of study at a school.

hair grower—A product of the Walker Company that relieved dandruff and other hair scalp disease.

National Association of Colored Women (NACW)—In 1896, several national groups of black women joined together under this name. They worked for equal rights for African Americans and women.

orphan—A child whose parents are both dead.

plantation—A large farm with hundreds of people who worked in the fields.

segregated—Separated from, apart. At one time, the United States had separate schools for blacks and whites.

self-made millionaire—A person who becomes very wealthy by earning money through her own business.

slaves—People who are owned by other people and forced to work without pay.

LEARN MORE

BOOKS

Aller, Susan Bivin. *Madam C. J. Walker*. Minneapolis: Lerner Classroom, 2007.

Hobkirk, Lori. *Madam C. J. Walker*. North Mankato, Minn.: Child's World, 2009.

Nichols, Catherine. *Madam C. J. Walker*. Danbury, Conn.: Children's Press, 2005.

WEB SITES

Madame C. J. Walker - Virtual Museum
<http://museum.madamewalker.net>

Madam C. J. Walker - The Official Web Site
<http://www.madamcjwalker.com>

INDEX